On poems in *Nothing But*

These poems '...have a freshnes[s]
sequence of poems dealing with
town in Ireland stands out in it[s]
of imagery.'

Alexandra Loske in The Frogmore Papers, *72, 2008*

'These are thoughtful and well-structured poems, with a down-to-earth voice that make subtle use of sound-patterns and line- and stanza-breaks, and some striking and memorable images. The reader has the feeling of having travelled some distance in a deceptively short and simple space.'

Susan Wicks

On poems in *Learning to Be English* and *Nothing But*

'So many of these poems are sharp and moving, richly suggestive with evocative details.'

Moniza Alvi

Maria C. McCarthy writes poetry, short fiction, reviews and memoir. She is currently working on a collection of linked short stories, *As Long As It Takes*, about first and second generation Irish women living in England. Some of these stories have been published by *The Frogmore Papers* and on the websites of *Writers' Hub* and *Tales of the Decongested*. She has also written and broadcast as a columnist for BBC Radio 4's *Home Truths* (as Maria Bradley).

She has an MA with Distinction in Creative Writing from the University of Kent.

She writes, and occasionally teaches creative writing, in a shed at the end of her garden in a village in North Kent.

www.medwaymaria.co.uk

strange
fruits

Also by Maria C. McCarthy

Nothing But (2007)
Learning to be English (2006, 2008)

strange
fruits

Maria C. McCarthy

WE ARE MACMILLAN.
CANCER SUPPORT

WordAid.org.uk

Cultured Llama Publishing

First published in 2011 for WordAid by
Cultured Llama Publishing
11 London Road
Teynham, Sittingbourne
ME9 9QW
www.culturedllama.co.uk

A CIP record for this book is available from The British Library

**All profits from the sale of this book go to Macmillan Cancer
Support, Registered Charity Number 261017**

For further information about this project and other WordAid
projects, please visit www.WordAid.org.uk

ISBN 978-0-9568921-0-2

Printed in Great Britain by Lightning Source UK Ltd

Contents

in memory of Karen McAndrew
Maria with Karen (right)

Preface

Karen McAndrew had little interest in my writing. I would tell her if I was taking a poetry class, doing a reading, but I never showed her my work, or talked about books with her. Our friendship was based on simple pleasures – cups and cups of tea, nattering about our families, 'mooching' around the charity shops of Rochester and pub lunches.

I haven't written a poem for Karen, but this collection opens with 'Blithe spirits', which Karen would have liked. Karen's blithe spirit will be wearing jeans, a brightly-coloured top with a bit of a sparkle on it and colourful jewellery, all found in charity shops. She may not bother with footwear now; she was a size 9 and had trouble finding fashionable shoes. Perhaps there is a plentiful supply of size 9s in the afterlife.

The collection closes with a prose piece, 'Where the High Street meets Star Hill', about our last outing together. May Karen be sitting in a cafe with an endless supply of tea, or in a pub, in good company, drinking Pernod and lemonade on ice from a tall glass.

Maria C. McCarthy

Foreword

This is the fourth project from WordAid, a collective of poets dedicated to raising money for charity (to date, over £4000) by publishing good writing. As in all our books, the poems here have been selected not only to make a positive impact on the world but because their quality brings its own rewards.

Maria McCarthy has dedicated this book to raising funds for Macmillan Cancer Support (www.macmillan.org.uk), the charity that helped her friend Karen McAndrew in the last weeks of her life and supported Karen's family and friends as they struggled to come to terms with their loss. Maria is a poet of remarkable skill, whose work offers surprising glimpses into our 21st-century lives – the 'strange fruits' of our civilisation or lack of it – shot through with meditations on the past and her heritage as 'an Irish girl, an English woman'. Whether describing a burnt-out building, 'its curved bones / bared like a half-carved turkey' or the dream-shop where 'the skins of outgrown friends / hung on a rack by the door', her images and insights are always unexpected and original. In 'Where the High Street meets Star Hill', she relates how she and Karen used to 'mooch' around charity shops, and Karen's gift for noticing items that she would reinvent as gifts for family and friends. Maria's parallel capacity to notice and reinvent the world around her in writing shines through in these pages.

Macmillan Cancer Support works with cancer sufferers and their relatives and friends to improve the lives of all those affected through providing practical, medical and financial support, as well as campaigning for better cancer care. Two million people in the UK are currently living with cancer and many of our lives have been touched by it, directly or indirectly, so there's no doubt this book will make a difference.

Buy it, enjoy the poems, and change lives for the better.

Vicky Wilson, WordAid.org.uk

Blithe spirits

Do women spirits glide ethereal
in chiffon, ectoplasm-green,
like in that Noel Coward film,
or do they haunt as when the angels came –
flannelette pyjamas; half-dressed
in bra and slip; safety pins clasping at
too-tight trousers – or well turned out
as for a viewing of the deceased?

Do they hobble round in slippers,
toes wrapped over toes,
or does the afterlife's chiropodist
pumice, balm, remould, render them to dance
in six-inch high stilettos, forever bunionless?

May yours be the marriage of voice and piano,
song and accompaniment, duet and solo,
sometimes soaring to top Cs,
sliding to changes of key with ease.

May there be light and shade to the music
of your marriage: the ambient sounds of a film;
the passion of opera; rock and punk
and jazz funk; singer-songwriter.

May you cover the best songs of others:
Joni, Eva, Regina, Half Man Half Biscuit.
May you work on your own songs,
husband and wife, music and lyrics.

*poem on the marriage of my daughter Rachel Bradley
to Stephen Morris, 22 January 2011*

Nice people

You drip into a puddle, but it's fine.
They get in such a muddle and you don't mind,
really, stepping from the shower to the phone,
because they're so nice.

You know that it'll build their confidence
if you can help to lift them from this mess,
that come next time they'll sort it out themselves;
you have faith in them.

You've so much more than they do; how could you complain?
Even as they're on your doorstep, sobbing,
interrupting the delicto you're enjoying.
It's just this once.

They've no-one else to go to, bless them,
and you're sure it won't happen again.

I dream of a shop filled with all the clothes I've ever worn

The shopkeeper offers the shirt
I wore on my eighteenth birthday –
the only gift I asked for –
blue and black, like a lumberjack's,

frayed threads, faded check,
detached collar and yoke
now healed. 'Try it on,' he tempts,
sleeve across breast, hand on heart.

It no more fits than the jeans
I wore with it – red-tagged,
stitched patch – the felt-penned plimsolls
lying gape-mouthed on the floor,

or the skins of outgrown friends
hung on a rack by the door.

After the fire at Matalan

Men in uniform lift and lower the tape
for other men in uniform
as the crane rises and circles.
Neighbouring stores close, choked by the acrid plumes,
bank holiday shoppers deprived of DIY and carpets.

And those of us housebound by the flames
walk by late afternoon to view the carcass
of this giant industrial bird, its curved bones
bared like a half-carved turkey,
and inhale charred remains that float,
then settle on the concrete of the retail park,
ochre insulation like discarded nesting.

Close to Christmas,
graffiti-ed hoardings disguise the deconstruction,
apologise for the inconvenience, while skip lorries
rattle the ashes of the pyre through the town.
Viewed through the square link fence,
an open space, a pile of rubble.

And still stray slices of the old bird's nest
skim the car park, perch on the branches of the winter trees.

Missed you on the day it rained

On the first day,
you lashed poles to poles,
vertical and horizontal,

created your own first floor with wooden planks,
filled in the cracks
in the brickwork.

You picked out the flowers and tendrils
on the lintels,
gold on brown,

and now you are painting the pillars
between the windows,
the rounded plinth

a rich chocolate, the column cream,
topped with the curves
of the fleur de lis.

I am learning the exact length and breadth
of the naked patch at the back of your head,
how it shines in the afternoon sun,

the way stray strands arch over
in the breeze
like a field of ripening corn.

If you would only turn round
you could see into my house.

Missed you on the day it rained.

April snow

Snow settles on the satellite
dish beneath the bedroom window
and on the supine tree in the garden below,
an unseasonal change from green to brown to white
since it was ousted on twelfth night.

You and I are propped in bed
checking emails on wireless internet,
browsing the broadsheets that tent our legs:
a pensioner busses from Penzance to Carlisle;
Heathrow's new terminal in terminal decline.

Later, my youngest flat-hunts online,
unlike you and I who trudged from window to window,
and I discover what my oldest is up to
by checking her status on Facebook:
Eating chocolate, staying home due to snow.

We reminisce about coal fires
that remained unlit till teatime,
the never-heated bedrooms,
and talk about lacing our boots,
making footprints, as I click the thermostat higher.

Railway cottages

Once a woman stood at this window
by a large stone sink
above a curtained cupboard,
and saw another at a window
loading sheets into a zinc bucket,
hauling them to the mangle in the yard.

She mirrored the other,
stepping from her own back door
with a basket of clothes
and a bag on a wooden hanger,
fashioned like a dress,
drawing pegs from the cleavage.

They chatted about drying, ironing, and
scrubbing grime from husbands' collars,
as they raised the washing skywards
with ropes and pulleys to wave
like flags at passing trains.
She kept a weather eye as

she billowed and straightened
sheets on children's beds,
and rushed out at the first spit
in a race with her neighbour,
draped clothes on an airer
to steam before the fire.

Night watch

I thought it dead, no sign of a leaf
until after the tulips had wizened beneath.

I am watching for a season –
a new gardener used to paving slabs and pots,
a townie come lately to a country plot –
and this tree appeared entombed in lichen.

Now, as the peonies shout as loud
as Ascot hats, a sudden budding.

Half-woken by an alien sound,
I peek through the curtain.

The tree glimmers; a portal through which princesses
may dissolve, returning at dawn with tattered slippers.

Now, to the daily watch
of the vegetable patch –
strawberries, courgettes, onion sets –
is added a night vigil,

waiting for the amber glow,
watching for a signal.

Strange fruits

Blackberries shrivel on Cellar Hill
though a few late blooms defy the new order:
bletted plums usurped by ripening pears.

A kestrel hovers over the orchard,
the gate staked by an estate agent's board.
Cobnuts lie scattered like popcorn on the turning

to Lynsted Lane, by the houses that first broke
through the earth in the spring, now de-scaffolded,
exhaling steam through plastic heating vents.

And strange fruits hang in the hedgerow,
Stella cans, a Co-operative bakery wrapper
with orange sticker, reduced to 40p.

Car on a country footpath

Twig fingers probe where windows
no longer wind down. Russet windfalls
tumble in the foot well, rot on skeletons of
once-upholstered seats. Long since scavenged
of mirrors, tyres, headlights, a bramble-clamped car
on a country footpath, though human-placed, is not out of place.
As much a part of the landscape now as the lines of planted poplars.

The brickbat wall

One side of a garden gate,
a man is building a wall
from threes and fours
and bits of bricks stuck
higgledy-piggledy,
tumbling-climbing,
upright crazy paving,
a never-identical twin
to the old wall
on the other side.

Can't get 'em now, says the builder,
meaning brickbats, rejects
from the brickfields of Conyer,
where men like him once worked,

so he makes his own,
with separate, perfect bricks,
cementing them to other perfect bricks,
breaking, mosaicing, tipping and turning.

Years ago I made a patchwork quilt.
Of old, scraps were clipped
from clothing, stitched by hand.
I cut my bedspread from bolts
of new material, machine-stitched
strips and stars and blocks,
perfect fabric re-imagined,
pretend make-do-and-mend.

How strange these crafts
of breaking and joining,
attempting the random,
recreation as recreation.

The old wall stands dark and mottled.
The new wall a uniform yellow,
like painting by numbers
with only one number.

At the Shrine of St Jude, Faversham

A kneeling bar, cushioned,
before a metal grille that shields
a statue; tealight candles, ten pence
a prayer; a pinboard of photos

of those for whom supplications
are offered – the sick, the dying –
and yellowed newspaper cuttings
of missing persons;

rosaries in plastic pots
like pill jars topped with figures
of St Jude, the near-forgotten apostle,
the patron saint of hopeless cases;

a poster for the visit of the relics
of a saint – Teresa's thigh and foot bones
in a jacaranda casket, cased in Perspex –
like Snow White's coffin – capable of healing.

St Teresa is on sale in the foyer,
cloak and halo iridescent on a card,
holy medal pinned above her prayer:
grant me the simplicity of a child.

Ghost writer

in memory of John Trelawny

You were slimmer, yes, and smaller
and your guttural growl restored
to before the cancer stole
the plums from your voice.

But then you were dead, in this dream,
returned to work on a piece of writing,
leaving its completion
to Nick Hornby and me.

I wouldn't have been your choice,
and Nick Hornby unlikely –
you would choose a writer of seafaring yarns,
smugglers' stories – but dreams have their own rules.

You were once told by our tutor
that you were a writer of popular
fiction, whilst I aspire to the literary,
working and reworking.

You wrote reams each week,
self-published, marketed,
sold and moved on. But now
you want me to edit your oeuvre.

Nick Hornby sits silently
throughout your visitation,
then half-smiles and stretches his arms,
his hands spaced the length,

breadth and depth of a box,
not visible, substantial,
and he lays the gift at my feet:
the secrets to completing

another man's work;
the secrets, in fact,
of writing.

Nick Hornby nods,
leaves, and you dissolve,
John. I am left with the box.

It's hard, the writing,
the rewriting,
the carrying on.

Remembrance

'Men marched on asleep. Many had lost their boots
But limped on, bloodshod.' Wilfrid Owen

A face freezes by the porthole glass,
barred entry for two minutes,
while we, who have chanced
on the scene, are forced into the service.

Head bowed, attempting reverence
I contemplate my shoelace,
and ponder the meaning of silence –
of how it never is – and think of John Cage

and his four minutes however many seconds.
A song dances in my head.
I cannot remember the dead,
distracted by the cut of women's skirts,

the design of a man's glasses,
the leaflets in the lobby
and the fact that the priest
read 'et' in the poem incorrectly,

the French way. Then I remember 'blood-shod',
and think of following the wagon with the dead,
and know the folly of the words, however read,
Dulce et decorum est pro patria mori.

Slipping down

Boxing Day, and when asked what you ate
for Christmas dinner you say,
'I should remember'.

You are slumped in a high-backed chair,
covered with a name-labelled blanket:
someone else's.

We are told that at the Christmas party
you boomed out the unerasable hymns,
rallied the others to sing.

Today you remember your daughter's face,
not her name; and of your son you inquire,
'Have we met?'

You search my face much longer than you
would have thought proper if you were not
as you are.

I am introduced, again, as 'Rob's friend.'
You scan from son to daughter,
and back again,

the half-formed thought refusing to set
like jelly made with too much water,
and you shout, 'I'll have to think about that.'

You've slipped further in your seat,
as your grandson does when watching TV.
Now it's Roger Moore as James Bond and

the woman in the red sweater wanders
in front of the screen and demands,
'Does anyone know what's supposed to happen?'

Your hands are bony thin; your thumbnail
thickened like a split hoof; and as you slip further
your shirt breaks free from belted trousers.

I have seen old photos, tie and jacket,
dapper. A care worker says
'We do put a tie on him,

'But there's health and safety to consider.
Joggers, that's what they need
when they get like that.'

Your skinny bottom changed by day
from too-loose pyjamas
to baby rompers.

Time to sit up for the latest snack: soup,
two triangles of bread and ham.
You are lifted by three tabarded women,

one at each arm, a third at your waist.
You growl as you are raised.
You want to be left to slip down.

Standards

He had a bee in his bonnet
about the state of public toilets
and the spongers on benefits.

His last words, to the tulips,
were, 'mustn't let my standards slip,'
concreting a small, important hole in the garden path.

He would have wanted it that way.

Blanket

You only had one pair,
and the devil makes work,
so you scrubbed, swept, polished,
baked in every inch of oven space,
rustled up stews and soups from scraps,
ripped stockings into strips, strapped
beans to poles, fruit to canes,

and by night you circled the square,
unravelled remnants of outgrown woollens
from long-forgotten photos –
shell-pink, peppermint, red-flecked beige –
hooked warmth into the holes,
edged it with a ribbed row of rust.

The ends still dangle: bitten, burnt,
sealed with a sliver of soap.

First supper

Large onion, tinned tomato,
add mince, crumble oxo,
simmer for ten mins or so.

Serve onto one plate,
one pyrex flan dish,
recipe etched on base.

Flank plate with knife
and fork, dish with
fork and spoon.

Add boyfriend,
stained carpet,
rented room.

Watch worms swim.
Read flan recipe
through mottled gravy.

Wish it was for mince.
Tip food in bin.

House

A van in the road, a couple shoulder
their mattress over a new threshold,
and I'm taken back to a Saturday in '88:
the furniture, that had filled our old flat, marooned.

We stretched into the new house,
hung the walls with images of ourselves
to look after the rooms when we were out,
coated the carpets with flakes of skin.

What happened between then
and the time when the bricks closed in?

Ten years since you left,
all rooms painted and papered.
Once in a while you slip through the letterbox.
The floorboards creak your name.

Coats

for Laura

There are seashells in this pocket,
trickling through collected silver
from thirds of pints of morning milk;
and in the other, a lone pineapple
chunk, stuck to the corner, and sugar
to chase with a licked finger.

Now the gabardine becomes a duffle
stuffed with bus tickets, folded into stars;
now, on a torn-off strip, a phone number
zipped within a denim bomber;
now an over-sized overcoat wrapped
around mother and unborn child,
now around mother and daughter.

Now she has her own coat.

Late

for Bob

You bustle past the window, strands flying
from your cap as if it were the only thing
holding your hair on, laptop bag slung

like a satchel, minus phone and wallet.
They are in that place you leave them
so you won't forget.

Your mother would have done this,
waved you down the road, noticed,
too late, your homework on the kitchen table.

Keats' House

The room in which we stand
has nothing to do with Keats,
built long after his death,

but within this extension
is Keats' front door,
and just along the corridor –

see, where the arch is – the divide
between Keats' and Fanny Brawne's
halves of the house –

the Brawnes had more
than half, actually.
There was a wall,

once, and a staircase,
since removed.
Not sure exactly where.

The chaise longue? No, it's not original.
We don't know Keats' taste in decor;
the themes of his poetry are love,

death and nature – not wallpaper.
And now we're in the Brawnes' parlour
where Keats first met Fanny. Possibly.

The items in the glass case are genuine –
Fanny's engagement ring, her scissors,
an inkstand, and the famous letters.

The plum tree?
Yes, that was where he wrote
Ode to a Nightingale.

No, not that tree;
that one's a facsimile.
And the garden is themed,

e.g. a flowerbed on melancholy.
The audio tour tells all,
playable as an MP3.

Don't forget Keats' death mask
in the bedroom, and his bust
in Fanny's parlour. He was very short,

you know, five foot and a quarter.
You wouldn't think it, would you?
For a poet of such stature.

Lager saga

Drunk young man on the rail replacement bus
slugging from your can of Tennant's lager,
yes, the bus was late. Why make such a fuss?

Your shouting does not endear you to us.
We will listen less as you grow louder,
drunk young man on the rail replacement bus.

Okay, we understand: you're furious.
(iPod's are found, volume turned up higher.)
Yes, the bus was late. Why make such a fuss?

The lack of trains makes you cantankerous,
but you will explode if you get redder,
drunk young man on the rail replacement bus.

Your railing makes us more impervious
to your complaints, yet you grow drunker.
Yes, the bus was late. Why make such a fuss?

Put your lager down; take several deep breaths;
relax. Have you thought of trying yoga,
drunk young man on the rail replacement bus?
Yes, the bus was late. Why make such a fuss?

In reply to your note

after William Carlos Williams

I don't keep
the best fruit
in the fridge
the taste of

the sun on
a ripe plum's
bloom is lost
when chilled

Forgive me
I've eaten
the sweetest
so warm so delicious

Shell

Spiral of pink-rinsed hair,
candy-striped twist of calcium thread,
coiled from point to miniature ear.

Fractal pendant, frilled-edged cameo,
stitched and quilted ribbon,
twisted strip of croissant dough.

Trumpet, horn of plenty, ice-cream cone,
washed-up shelter for a creature
long gone.

Salt and pepper

I won it at a funfair,
a salt and pepper set.
Keep it for your bottom drawer,
my mother said.

I was eight.
No marriage plans as yet.

Photo

A beach, Lahinch,
1974, I think.

I'm wearing tank top,
skirt, platforms, tights, no

smile, head to one side,
and there's my father,

on the same sea wall
yards away, miles away,

head turned the other way,
in suit and tie.

Mitchelstown – a sequence

I   The road to Mitchelstown

Suitcases were suitcases then:
large and square, with plastic grips.

They could only be carried a few steps –
one shoulder stooped,
the other raised –
then dropped, hands flexed,
and picked up again
as on the road to Calvary.

So many years I've held the memory
of sailing to Dun Laoghaire
with my mother,
left with the luggage
while she searched for something lost.

Ireland rose in the morning
after the cold crossing on the open deck
of the Hibernian: a passage of women
and children in new clothes,
bags for beds, jackets for pillows.

Once we reached my mother's home
each relative, school, old house, gravestone
was visited and venerated
like the Stations of the Cross.

The suitcases were lighter coming back:
gifts of clothing we'd outgrown
passed on to younger cousins.

This year
I pack four new pairs of knickers,
four of socks, one for each day,
as was done for me
when my clothes were mixed
with my brothers' and sisters'.

Though it's taken all of my forty-seven years
to reach my father's birthplace,
it's all too easy now I'm on my way:

no rise and fall of the ferry,
no full day's travel from Euston to Holyhead,
Holyhead to Dun Laoghaire,
Dublin to Clare;

it's less than an hour by Aer Lingus,
baggage checked at Heathrow,
returned on the carousel at Cork.
It's like eating Easter eggs
without living through Lent.

I wheel my suitcase behind me
and take a seat on Bus Eirann,
from the Parnell Place Coach Station,
Route 8 to Mitchelstown.

My father found the strength
to lift his bags off at this stop
just three times in over fifty years.

I bear no gifts, only photographs
to show those who might remember,
may know what I wish to learn.

I don't know yet if my luggage
will be lighter or heavier
on my return.

II My father's house

'My daddy lived here.'
I lean towards the boy
who shelters in his father's shadow.

We perform the photographic ritual,
standing by the door where he once stood,
the same height as this child.

Two rooms, turf fire, one oil lamp.
Water carried in barrels by donkey and cart.
There are extensions now, bedrooms, kitchen, bathroom.

'I was reared here too,' says Nelly,
gripping the hand of the younger man.
'Your grandfather taught my grandfather to dance.'

'Poor times,' says Jimmy
behind the steering wheel
where he has remained since driving us here
at twenty miles an hour,
worried by the new road that cuts
through Carthy's burreen,
unused to roundabouts.

Flying out and flying home,
an empty seat beside me.
Flying home and flying back,
he's let me have the window.

III Not even trying

Some speak well of them
as they would of the dead.

'Presentation Convent' wrought in iron
spans the gates in a half moon,
and a plaque commemorates the order,
moved on in favour of new development –
a cinema, a leisure centre –
the rooms behind the boarded windows
haunted by just four women at its closure.

Were they the good ones,
the balance on the scales?

Their children learnt the petitionary prayer:
Please God, not me. The child in the next chair,

afraid to raise his hand, afraid to not raise his hand,
beaten for getting it wrong, beaten for not even trying.

IV Windowless

There was light enough that night.

I can only guess
if my great aunt's hair was red,
her dress blue or brown
as she stood at the foot of the town
in the heat of the patriot's flames,
not knowing that children to come
would tell her tale to a newfound cousin
with vowels like the Kingstons
who had crowned an Irish town
with an English castle.

Built in the image of Windsor,
'Just one window less',
I am told more than once,
wondering how the light came in,
mistaking it for 'windowless'.

V   Two women

We searched the stones
for names that matched our own.
Two women, just met, in the graveyard
of the Church of the Immaculate Conception.

'They'd money to build in spite of the famine.'
you said, nodding towards the date engraved
on the tower: 1847.

I told you of my recent find,
a certificate of baptism.
'My father was a "boy child",

raised by his mother's sister.'
A similar fate
had befallen your grandmother.

The unwed mothers fled:
one to England, one to America.

We entered the church together,
new-found companions,
English-Irish, Irish-American,

descendants of the country that dispersed
its fallen women to one of three destinations:
England, America, the sisters of Magdalene,

and I pictured a girl at the altar,
offering her child
to be cleansed of Original Sin,

handing him to her sister.
Leaving.

VI Completely

My blood is vintage Irish
but my accent is a giveaway:
Chatham, South East London, Surrey,
with sounds of Counties Cork and Clare.

At grammar, university,
I learnt an English history –
the coming of the railroad,
the growth of industry –
came lately to the famine road,

yet I'm steeped in Latin Credo,
a dose of mea culpa, Agnus Dei,
and choruses of rebel songs
performed at home,
withheld from English company.

In my twenties I received an
English name, swallowed it whole
like the body of Christ.
In my forties, spat it out –
learnt to sign as myself again.

I'm Irish with an English voice,
English with an Irish heart,
floating forever between
Holyhead and Dun Laoghaire,

an Irish girl, an English woman,
not half and half: completely.

* * *

Our Father

Our Father, who is in Heaven, you gave us
our crisps and a bottle of R White's
on a Friday night. We knelt by the bed,
hands pressed: *forgive us our trespasses*,
before we could know what trespasses meant.

Harder to pray when you slipped
from the pew to the call of the glass,
the first drawn pint after evening Mass.
I would go up to receive and return
from the rail to an empty seat.

Did the Lord forgive as you filtered
your trespasses? Forgive, as I refused
to utter your prayer? Sleep in peace,
Our Father, all trespasses forgiven.

Story

I know this story:

it's one of nuns and Christian brothers;
    of drawing water from a well; of winters
        without shoes; of delivering your sister

when the midwife couldn't come; of finding
    a man in the barn, hanging; of sailing
        on the open deck of the night boat

to Holyhead with one suitcase, bearing
    two of everything; of working in a hospital; of sending
        money home; of cinemas and dancehalls and clinging

to your own; of meeting my father
    at a dance above the Gas Showrooms;
        of the pale blue wedding dress (four months gone);

of leaving the reception while he stayed on,
    drinking; of living with his mother
        who complained about a mark on the wall

made by the touch of the baby's fingers;
    of moving to a hostel whilst waiting to be housed
        (no men allowed); of travelling to Ireland

with my brother; of the farmer
    who would've taken you on, mother and son;
        of the older man in England, who courted

you before you met my father, who treated
    you to a show, Chu Chin Chow on ice,
        who walked his dog past our house

every day until he died, the house the council gave
    you once you had five, where my father
        led you a hell of a life with the drink

and the babies and the miscarriage;
    of the doctor who treated you like
        you'd brought it on yourself; of hiding

from the rent man; of us all turned out nice,
    hair brushed, clean socks, so the neighbours
        wouldn't know; of how did it for us,

stayed with a man
    who was only home
        when the pubs closed,

or the horses ran
    the wrong way.
        I know this story;

it's yours, not mine. I've stopped listening.

July 1969

One small school is gathered for assembly
in the sun-freckled shade of the chestnut tree.
Sister Bernadette, haloed by the sun
like a statue of the Virgin, says Class One,
just like the men who have walked on the moon,
will take their own small steps soon.
They will not return to skewer conkers
from St Joseph's tree, but, come September,
step up to St Andrew's or the grammar.
Except Michael Sullivan who will never
grow into his too-big blazer, unworn
in an unopened wardrobe. Picture his step
from behind the ice-cream van, like the boy
in the road safety poster: frozen, poised.

Survival

Her scales tear layer from layer, and she
slithers into clothing to conceal the sheen of skin:
shimmering purples, pearl and green.

'Looking for business?' the human asks.
'My God, you're cold,
as cold as the sea. My God, My God,' he gasps,

but God can't save him now.
He has dropped his coins in the mermaid's purse:
the King's shilling in reverse.

Those that were his feet, now fins. His legs conjoin.
She leaves him at the harbour wall,
a convert to the mermaid's cause: survival.

Dentists – a sequence

I   Dental treats

Five siblings,
each opened wide
while the others waited

nicely. We were famed
for good behaviour.
The receptionist

remarked on it
every six months.
Mother glowed.

Checked-up, we'd scamper,
pennies in our pockets,
to the sweet shop next door,

a reward for Mother's pride.

II Mr O'Riordan was Australian

He had a cartoon in his reception –
of him and his partner standing at windows,
a patient apiece reclined in chairs, string
knotted to teeth, a brick in one dentist's hand.
In Mr O'Riordan's, a boomerang.

III   The one whose eyes sparkled above his mask

Handsome as a doctor on television,
he set this woman's heart a-racing.

IV   Toffee

Everlasting toffee strips;
Bluebird slabs cracked with a hammer;
I was a frequent flier in the dentist's chair,
and a chocolate eclair did for one tooth,
the lump I couldn't swallow not its creamy centre
but the broken shard of a molar.

The dentist said he'd see toffee banned.
That, and free treatment for immigrants.

V Extractions

There was another – tugging on a rotten
molar took two hours with a sobbing break.
Next time I begged for general anaesthesia.

She asked me to write a poem
to frame for the waiting room.

Inspiration never came.

   * * *

Hairdressers, or affairs of the hair

The one before was an alcoholic.
The bastard left me colourless the week
before the wedding, didn't show up. Well,

I fell into the hands of another.
It could have been disastrous: either
as one-off encounter or regular affair. We're

heading for our second anniversary,
Bob and I, me and Sam. Happy? Very.

Raising poems

There is a quickening early in the day.
This is a delicate time with singing
and dancing, or an inability to rise,
and what has arrived can as soon be lost.

It's ages before you can leave them alone.
You must feed them, even when exhausted.
Partners grow to know that distracted moan,
the paraphernalia beside the bed,
the way you slip from their arms at dawn.
They learn to be second best.

Some of them you cannot live with.
You hide them in drawers
to be discovered, perhaps,
after your death.
Imagine the gasps,
'How could she?'

Those that survive you must let go.
You regard them from a distance: notice,
too late, that they're not dressed right.
They are no longer yours.
There is nothing you can do.

Where the High Street meets Star Hill

We meet for coffee at half ten in Norma's Cafe, where they have tables outside and Karen can smoke. We catch up on some of our news, then hit the charity shops: Mind, British Red Cross, Oxfam, Barnardos, and by that time it's twelve, and Ye Arrow is open for lunch. We have vegetable wraps and chips at £4.95. This is the first time Karen eats that day, as she doesn't do breakfast, but she will have filled up on tea and cigarettes during the morning.

I've suggested eating somewhere different, something different. We went to the Eagle once – my treat, as I was flush – and had two meals for £8, fish and chips. She said she liked it, at the time, but the next time we met she said she didn't really, and we went back to Ye Arrow. So if I get tired of the same pub, the same meal, I order different food.

Karen drinks Pernod and lemonade on ice in a tall glass. Sometimes I have fizzy water, sometimes dry white wine, occasionally a half of cider. The last of these surprised her, when we last ate out. She'd never known me to drink cider. I like a change; Karen likes things to stay the same.

In the summer, we sit outside in the smokers' area. When it's cold or wet we sit indoors, and Karen nips out for a cig. We admire each other's charity shop bargains, catch up on how things are with my other half and my daughters, her other half and her sons. Sometimes I complain about this and that; Karen rarely does.

After lunch, we do the charity shops at the other end of the High St: Hospices of Hope, Sue Ryder and Cancer Research. Hospices of Hope has a bargain rail outside, £1 an item. Karen rummages through this while I look inside, then she catches me up. She likes the bric-a-brac as well as the clothes. She finds things that other people would like: for her neighbour that keeps all the cats and has Alzheimer's; for her friend that drinks, but has spells on the wagon; Christmas and birthday presents for friends and family, which she buys all year round and keeps for the right occasion. For herself, she buys jeans and tops with a bit of sparkle on them, sequins and studs; things for her kitchen; bits of furniture for her home. Sometimes the things she buys are too heavy or bulky for her to carry, and she leaves them to be collected by her boyfriend.

I like to be in good time for my train, so we say good-bye ten minutes before it's due, standing outside the shop that sells flowers on one side and work boots on the other, where the High Street meets Star Hill. It's a quick peck on the cheek, a smile, and a promise to meet again in a few weeks.

We don't meet in August. When I call at the end of the month, Karen says she's been in hospital and doesn't know why. Her boyfriend had found her unconscious, at home, and called an ambulance. She was 'out of it' on the ward, confused. Karen has mental health problems, and has spells in hospital, but this sounds different. She doesn't want to arrange for us to meet; she is too tired to go out. I have a minor operation lined up in September, so we agree to meet when I've recovered, when Karen has regained some energy.

At the end of October I get an email from a member of Karen's family. Karen is in hospital. It's cancer, malignant tumours in her stomach and liver. I see her in hospital, thin and weak but cheerful, as is her way. We joke that we have both complained about gaining weight, we missed our skinny days, but this isn't the way to do it.

November, two weeks on from diagnosis, she is home, and my husband Bob and I arrive to take her out to Norma's cafe. She is skeletal, yellow-tinged, wonders whether she'll be able to make it to the car, to the cafe, but some-how we get there. Two cappucinos, mine a decaff, and she fancies a packet of Quavers, so that's what I get her. She is exhausted after twenty minutes, so Bob goes to get the car, to bring it as close as possible. She asks to sit outside in the cold air. She has spent weeks indoors, staring out the window, too tired for TV, bored of the radio. 'I do love you, Karen,' I say. She giggles. She and I don't say things like that to each other. 'I love you too,' she says, and gives me a peck on the cheek.

I doubt that we'll do the charity shops again, Karen and I. If we ever do, I shan't complain about going to Ye Arrow, about having vegetable wraps and chips again. Just one more time would be enough: Pernod and lemonade on ice in a tall glass for Karen; dry white wine for me. Outside, so Karen can have a ciggie. One more peck on the cheek when we say goodbye, where the High Street meets Star Hill.

Karen McAndrew died two weeks after our outing.
This book is dedicated to her memory.

Notes and acknowledgements

Some poems from this collection have been published in the following magazines: *Conversation Poetry Quarterly*; *14*; *The Frogmore Papers*; *Equinox*, *Teynham News* and *The New Writer*. Some poems have been published in *Night Train 5*, University of Kent, 2007; *On the Line*, Canterbury City Press, 2010; *Canterbury Poet of the Year*, Canterbury Festival, 2010; and in the pamphlets *Nothing But* (2007) and *Learning to be English* (2006, 2008) by Maria C. McCarthy.

'July 1969' was shortlisted for the Frogmore Poetry Prize, 2006, highly commended in the Split the Lark poetry competition, 2007 and longlisted for the MsLexia poetry competition, 2007. 'Standards' and 'July 1969' were part of a submission that was shortlisted for the T.S. Eliot Poetry Prize, University of Kent, 2006. 'At the Shrine of St Jude, Faversham' was highly commended in the Save As poetry competition, 2010. Maria achieved second place for 'Story' in Canterbury Festival Poet of the Year, 2010.

Mitchelstown – a sequence

In February 2007, at the age of 47, Maria travelled to her father's hometown of Mitchelstown, Co. Cork, for the first time. She is grateful to Liam Cusack for his time and efforts before and during the trip, for local and historical detail of Mitchelstown, for helping her to find the boy her father was, and so to understand the man that he became.

'Windowless' refers to the burning of Mitchelstown Castle, Co. Cork, in 1922, at the end of the Irish War of Independence. Mitchelstown Creameries, known locally as the Co-op, acquired the site and, later, built a milk-processing factory on the exact location where the castle once stood.

In 'Two women', a child born out of wedlock was known as 'a boy child' or a 'girl child'.

'Mitchelstown – a sequence' is dedicated to Jim McCarthy, 1928–2000.

'Ghost Writer' is in memory of John Trelawny, with whom Maria took the MA in Creative Writing at the University of Kent, 2005–2007. He was an avid self-published author, his most successful work being *The Islanders*, Beavers' Press, 2007. Although he professed to 'not really understand poetry' (usually when asked to look over some of Maria's draft poems), he was no mean poet himself, published in *Logos*, *Conversation Poetry Quarterly* and in the *Night Train* series of anthologies.

Thanks are due to Bob Carling, who edited and designed this collection, to Maggie Drury for cover images, logo and encouragement, to the WordAid poets, and to all those who commented on these poems during their gestation and delivery: the MA in Creative Writing class at the University of Kent, 2005–2007; tutors Susan Wicks and Patricia Debney; and members of the 'Best Words, Best Order' and 'Small' poetry classes taught by Maria in 2009 and 2011.

Lightning Source UK Ltd.
Milton Keynes UK
UKOW042236210613

212661UK00001B/5/P